Reconsidered

What the Bible Actually Says
About a Woman's Role in Church

Russ Adcox

RECONSIDERED

What the Bible Actually Says About a Woman's Role in Church

Copyright 2021 © Russ Adcox

ISBN 978-1-387-76591-1

All Scripture quotations, unless otherwise indicated, are taken from the Holy Bible, New International Version®, NIV®. Copyright ©1973, 1978, 1984, 2011 by Biblica, Inc.™ Used by permission of Zondervan. All rights reserved worldwide. www.zondervan.com The "NIV" and "New International Version" are trademarks registered in the United States Patent and Trademark Office by Biblica, Inc.™

All rights reserved. No part of this book, including icons and images, may be reproduced in any manner without the prior written permission from the copyright holder, except where noted in the text and in the case of brief quotations embodied in critical articles and reviews.

Cover artwork and design by Scott Utter
Interior by Good Sign Design Co.

Printed in the United States of America.

Dedication

To my daughters, Lilly and Halle, may you never live in a world where your voice is silenced, ignored, or discredited in the church.

TABLE OF CONTENTS

Acknowledgments	5
Introduction	7
Four Disclaimers	11
The Times Have Changed	15
My History with Women's Role	21
Women in the Creation Story	29
Women in the Old Testament	35
Women in the Time of Jesus	39
Women in the New Testament Church	45
Should Women Remain Silent?	53
Are Women Permitted to Teach?	67
Concluding Reminders	77
Works Referenced and Resources for Further Study	80

ACKNOWLEDGMENTS

I never intended for this little book to become an actual book. First, it was a Bible study with my elders, then a sermon series, then a series of articles, etc. The fact it became a book is thanks to the countless people who heard me stumble through the early sermons, teachings, and drafts. These include the elders who first walked with me through the study in 2010 – Gary VanWormer, Alex Domkowski, Max Boren, Buddy Norman, and the late Stephen Worley and Harold Clark. All fine men, dedicated Christians, and astute Bible scholars. They challenged my thinking on numerous points.

I am indebted to Rubel Shelly and Mike Cope. Both are outstanding thinkers within the Churches of Christ and they had a major influence on this work. Their sermons on this topic (which are no longer available online) had a significant influence on my sermons. It is likely I sometimes quote them in this book without realizing I am quoting them and thus, fail to give them proper credit. I hope they understand.

I also thank the members of the Maury Hills Church for their graciousness, patience, and challenge. They listened, ask questioned, pushed back, and walked through the Scriptures with me. There are far too many to name, but I am thankful for each and every one.

Finally, I must thank a few people who helped bring this book to reality. Gary Vanwormer, Ashleigh Givens, and Ebony Lovely read the rough draft, provided theological feedback, and grammatical corrections. Scott Utter created the cover design and layout. And the always creative Todd Loyd suggested the title.

I would be remiss if I did not thank you for reading this book! I am honored and humbled you chose to engage this text. Regardless of where you will fall out (in agreement, disagreement, or still not quite sure) I thank you for reading and thinking critically about this important topic.

INTRODUCTION

Does the world really need another book on women's role? No. Many authors of much greater theological heft than I have undertaken the task. So, why this book? Why dedicate time and resources to a topic already covered in such depth? And one which is, admittedly, not central to the core teachings or practice of the Christian faith?

First, this book was written to help the church I serve better understand the teachings of the Bible on this topic. I have served as the Lead Pastor of Maury Hills Church in Columbia, TN since 2004. The church launched three years earlier in 2001 with a simple desire to be non-denominational and non-judgmental. It also sought to be a safe place for people to ask questions and explore faith. This was particularly important to the topic of women's role because our church has roots in the Churches of Christ (as do I) and those churches have historically taken a very conservative view of women's role.

In the early years of Maury Hills, a woman could not lead any activity of the assembly. They did not offer public prayers, lead worship, read Scripture, offer communion thoughts, or preach. They could not even make announcements or serve communion. Of course, women did many of these things in Bible classes or small groups, but the main assembly was strictly limited to male leadership. This was also true of other leadership roles in the church. It was not weird or unusual to us. It was simply the way we had always done things.

However, in 2010, our church changed its position. After an exhaustive study of the Scriptures, we began to open more leadership roles to women and invite their full participation in the assembly. We came to believe we had mis-understood and mis-applied much of the Bible's teaching on women's role. Today women offer prayers, lead worship, read Scripture, give communion thoughts, and preach at Maury Hills. We also have women who serve as ministry team leaders and pastors. Currently, four of the eight ministers on staff are women and one regularly preaches on Sundays.

This still creates some discomfort among new members and attenders because many of them also grew up in the Churches of Christ or denominations with similar positions on women's roles (i.e. Southern Baptist or Pentecostal). So, I still get questions, and it is hard to unpack years of teaching into one conservation after Sunday services or one reply to a Monday morning email. It is my hope this book will help people understand why we changed our views on women's role and what the Bible actually says about it.

However, this is not just a book for the Maury Hills Church. After offering a refresher course in Fall of 2020, I realized many others have an interest in the topic. Some grew up in denominations like mine and struggle to reconcile their current beliefs with past teachings. They have since changed their views on women's role, but are still not sure how it squares with passages like 1st Corinthians 14 or 1st Timothy 2. Others are still wrestling through the question and not sure what their views are. They simply want to know what God's Word has to say about it.

I also realized many of the books dedicated to this topic address it from a purely theological standpoint. While I deal with those questions in the book, I also talk about how our church navigated this issue moving from a strict complementarian position to a more open stance. I hope this is helpful to other churches who may be moving in the same direction (or members of similar churches). In this sense, the book is not just for my church, it is for the church as a whole. Regardless of your background, denomination, beliefs, or current position on women's role, I hope you will benefit from our journey together.

FOUR DISCLAIMERS

Considering the controversial nature of this topic, I do not expect all of us will agree. There are simply too many opinions and views for 100% agreement. So, before we get too far down the road together, let me offer a few disclaimers:

1. There are many different opinions on this topic. Not only within Christianity as a whole, but also within the church I serve. There are two main views of women's role in Christendom and dozens of nuances in between. Every one of them are represented in my church (and yours). This fact alone should give us pause and prevent us from holding our own positions too dogmatically.

2. Our opinions on this topic are mostly influenced by the church of our childhood. The teachings of the church in our formative years largely shaped the way we interpret the key passages on women's role. Since most of us have not undertaken a serious study of the

topic, this view is probably still our view. Put simply, we believe what we were taught to believe. This is not a criticism, just reality.

3. Even if we've since changed our opinion on it, or at least become more open to a different understanding, there is a big difference between changing our mind intellectually and accepting it emotionally. The first time I preached on this topic I received an email from one of our long-time members who said, "I've carefully studied the Scriptures with you and have come to many of the same conclusions. They are logical, practical, and Biblical. But my heart will not let me accept them yet and my stomach still churns in worship." I understood exactly what she meant.

4. It should be recognized that the Bible must be interpreted, and interpretation is no easy task. Sincere students of Scripture often reach different conclusions on controversial issues. They do so while maintaining equal respect for the authority and inspiration of God's Word.

Therefore, when it comes to women's role, I appeal to the old Restoration Movement motto:

In matters of faith, unity;
In matters of opinion, liberty;
In all things, love.

I have no problem fellowshipping with, worshiping with, or being members of the same congregation with brothers and sisters who see the issue differently than me. I believe there is room for different views and interpretations. We should never allow our understanding of controversial issues like this to come between our common faith in Christ. After all, we are on the same team! While we may not agree on this issue, we agree on what matters most and that is enough for unity.

THE TIMES HAVE CHANGED

A few generations ago Bob Dylan famously sung, *"the times they are a'changin.'"* Well, they have a'changed! Cultural views on women in the 1950s and 60s are drastically different than 2020 and beyond. There is an old clip from *Leave it to Beaver* where Wally is helping Ward grill hamburgers. He naively asks his dad, *"Why do men do all the cooking outside and women do all the cooking inside?"* Ward smiles and answers, *"Well you know how they say a woman's place is in the home? Well, if she's going to be in the home, she might as well be in the kitchen."*

Go ahead. Try that line out today. Times have clearly changed. 100 years ago, in this country, women could not vote or hold elected office. If they were married, they could not own property, make legal contracts or divorce an abusive husband. They had limited opportunities for higher education and were often forbidden from pursuing a career outside the home. The dominant view of women was their place was in the home and their primary function was wife and mother. There was no need for education or leadership training because women were expected to stay "in their place." They were viewed as the "weaker sex" and inferior to men in terms of intellect, abilities, business acumen, work skills, aptitude, etc.

What is striking is this view of women continued to dominate American culture decades after women's suffrage movement of the 1920s. It continued to dominate well in the 1940s when World War II and Rosie the Riveter brought women into the workforce in large numbers. It continued through the Civil Rights era of the 1960s which brought laws making it unlawful to discriminate on the basis of gender. It even continued well into my childhood of the 1980s.

When I was a kid, I attended a church camp at Freed Hardeman College called "Future Church Leaders Workshop." It was only for boys. They taught us how to preach three-point sermons, keep 4/4-time, read Scripture, and lead public prayer. We were encouraged to grow up and become elders, deacons, and ministers in the church. They had a separate camp for girls where they were taught none of these things. They were encouraged to serve in less public roles and be supportive wives of elders, deacons, and ministers. To the boys the message was, "one day you can grow up and be a *leader* in the church." To the girls the message was, "one day you can grow up and *marry* a leader in the church." This was not that long ago and, thankfully, much has changed.

Today, women have equal rights with men and equal opportunity. Women serve as doctors, lawyers, soldiers, professors, CEOs, presidents, governors, senators, etc. (all professions that were once considered off limits). They can pursue college degrees and are seen as equally intelligent and capable. To say otherwise is considered chauvinistic or discriminatory. Within the last century, there has been a significant shift in terms of how we treat women and view their role in society. This change in attitude has gradually forced the church to deal with the issue as well.

Fifty years ago, to explain the church's restrictions on women in leadership was more accepted because it more closely mirrored society-at-large. This is no longer the case. How do you explain to a woman CEO that her leadership skills are not needed in the church? Or she cannot lead a ministry because she lacks the necessary qualifications? How do you explain to a female college professor that she can teach male and female students 40 hours out of the week but during that one hour on Sunday she must remain silent? Regardless of what you believe about this issue, you have to admit the church's traditional stance is becoming increasingly difficult to accept in modern society.

Rubel Shelly correctly observed:

> *"It is an undeniable fact that changes in our culture raise questions for the church to address. It is neither practical nor right to pretend these questions are unworthy of consideration. There is no virtue in a closed mind, and the world will never take a religion seriously that cannot address its current concerns."*

It is not wrong for Christians to take questions of culture seriously. Of course, this does not mean we allow culture to dictate our answers to these questions. We live under the authority of God's Word. Where culture and God's Word disagree, we side with the Word of God. But in cases where the prevailing sentiment and Scripture agree, we may move with the culture. The sad reality is sometimes the culture has been right, and the church has been wrong.

For example, look at Southern white churches during the Civil Rights Movement. Culture forced these churches to deal with the issue of racism. They did not initiate the change on their own. Societal pressure forced them to open their Bibles and do more research. It forced them to rethink the traditional interpretations that were once used to defend segregation. The point is simply sometimes our tried and tested interpretations do not stand up to scrutiny and, in such cases, we must rethink our position and ask if it is consistent with the Word of God.

This is exactly what we will do in this book. Yes, we will deal with the controversial passages everyone likes to quote when the issue comes up, but we will also spend considerable time looking at the story of women in the larger story of the Bible. Our views on this subject, or any subject, should not be formed by a handful of verses alone. They should be formed on the teaching of the whole Bible. We will get there shortly, but first a bit more of my story.

DISCUSSION QUESTIONS

1. How has society's attitude towards a woman's role changed in your lifetime?

2. How has the church responded to these changes in culture? How should we respond?

3. The culture in which we're trying to apply the Bible (the 21st century) is obviously very different from the culture in which it was written (the 1st century). How does this affect our understanding and application of Scripture? What factors should we consider when weighing cultural changes against the Word of God?

MY HISTORY WITH WOMEN'S ROLE

To tell my story, I need to define a couple of terms—egalitarian and complementarian. These are the two primary views of women's role in the church today. Both are based on careful study of the Scriptures, and both are held by Bible-believing Christians.

- **Egalitarian**—those who believe there is equal ministry opportunity for both genders (i.e. women can serve in any role in the church in which a man can serve, there are no limits or restrictions). They generally appeal to Galatians 3:26-28.

- **Complementarian**—those who believe ministry roles are differentiated by gender (i.e. there are certain roles for men and certain roles for women, thus there are some restrictions on leadership roles for women). They generally appeal to 1st Corinthians 14:34-35 and/or 1st Timothy 2:12-14.

Within complementarianism there is also a wide range of beliefs. There are progressive complementarians who believe in differing roles for men and women, but think the differences are limited to a rather small subset. For example, they may believe a woman can do anything in the church except preach or serve as a pastor. Then there are strict complementarians who say a woman is forbidden from any type of leadership role in the church or assembly with no exceptions. Progressive complementarians tend to lean more on 1st Timothy 2:12 while strict complementarians lean more on 1st Corinthians 14:34.

My history is with the latter. I grew up in a conservative Church of Christ. We were strict complementarians, although we did not know to call it that. We just called it "doing what the Bible said." Women held no leadership positions in our church, and they were not allowed to do anything in the Sunday worship assembly. Growing up I never once heard a woman speak from the pulpit in the auditorium. No teaching, no prayers, no reading of Scripture, no announcements. Nothing. They were to "remain silent." Of course, women taught every one of my Sunday school classes but only until the 5th grade. Once the boys started getting baptized, women were no longer allowed to teach them (as if baptism was somehow a mark of "manhood").

I was in my 20s before I heard a woman pray publicly (and it probably offended me at the time). I was in my 30s before I heard a woman lead worship or preach in the assembly (it did not offend me by then but it sure made me uncomfortable). I know it sounds like an exaggeration. It is not. Allowing women to speak in an assembly was like breaking one of the Ten Commandments. It was ignoring the *clear command* of

God. After all, hasn't everyone read 1st Corinthians 14 and 1st Timothy 2?

The Maury Hills Church started in the same way with women's role. Maybe not as strict as the church of my childhood, but since we began as a Church of Christ we largely assumed the same historic position of those churches regarding women's role. Women had a very limited role in our assemblies. They did not read Scripture, pray, teach, or serve communion. They could serve on the praise team, but only if seated on the front row. We also allowed women to serve as *ministry leaders* but not *deacons*. This was a creative side-step in semantics. Ministry leaders served the exact same role as deacons, but we called the men deacons and the women ministry leaders. We were more open to women's leadership in areas outside of the assembly. They often read Scripture, prayed, and taught in small groups or Bible classes. But overall, we maintained a fairly conservative position on women's role.

There was one important distinction. We openly acknowledged many of our practices were based on tradition rather than Scripture. We also pledged to do a more thorough study at some point to see how well our position aligned with Scripture. We started that study in 2009. Our elders spent a couple of days studying it together at their annual retreat and held many future conversations and discussions in our weekly meetings. After a period of study and prayer, they asked me to lead the church through a study in 2010. This included a seven-week teaching series and small group studies.

We did not set out to change anything. We just wanted to check our traditions and practices against Scripture. Over the course of the study, we concluded we had mis-interpreted and mis-applied the two key texts that seem to prohibit women's role. We also realized the Biblical picture was much broader and more open than those verses alone. Thus, we ended up changing our position to reflect a more open stance.

In 2010, we communicated our position in this way:

> "At Maury Hills, we believe a woman can participate in any activity of the assembly and serve in any capacity in the church, with the exception of an Elder or Senior Minister."

We included the Senior Minister position not because the role involved preaching, but because the Senior Minister operated much like an Elder in our governance model. This distinction created confusion later as many believed we had "changed our position" when we begin asking women to preach in 2019. Yes, it took us nine years to fully implement our changes!

Immediately after the 2010 study, women began leading various activities in the assembly (public prayers, reading Scripture, serving communion, etc.). Within a couple of years, we also hired our first female minister and promoted our long-time church secretary to the role of Member Care Minister. We allowed everything except preaching and our reasoning was simple. We did not think the church was ready for it. Many of the above changes were already a stretch for members who had grown up as strict complementarians, so we thought preaching would have to wait. We believed it was Scriptural, just not practical for our church at the time. The confusion came once we decided it was time to invite women to preach. Some quickly responded with, "but I thought we said they couldn't be a Senior Minister?!" In hindsight, we should have done more teaching/explanation on this.

Of course, we lost some members over the changes (as I'm sure you can imagine), but not as many as we feared. Most were willing to listen and give space for their thoughts/opinions to form. Some found the study convicting and changed their position with us. Some were not quite as convicted, but still did not believe the issue was one they wanted to leave the church over. They were willing to endure a little discomfort in the assembly to maintain unity with their brothers and sisters.

One of my favorite stories from this time was from a member who approached me in the hallway the day I wrapped up the series and said, *"Russ, I disagree with every word you said in that series… but I love you… and I'm leaving."* She hugged me and left. It was bittersweet because she was more than a member, she was a family friend, but I understood her struggle. She did not agree and was not sure she would ever be comfortable in worship again. She did not leave angry and upset. She left with grace. After six months she was back. She said, *"I discovered something from visiting other churches. There's something I disagree with at every one of them. So, I figured if I was going to attend an imperfect church, it might as well be this one."*

Her story is one of Christian maturity. She was willing to set aside her personal preferences for the larger mission of the church. I pray more would have the courage to do so. She was also willing to listen and examine the Scriptures for herself. While we did not agree on everything in the end (and still don't), we do agree this issue does not rise to the level of breaking fellowship with each other. We may never see eye-to-eye on women's role, but we see eye-to-eye on Christ and that is enough.

With that said, let us start our journey together at a good place—the beginning.

DISCUSSION QUESTIONS

1. What were the attitudes/practices of the church you grew up in regarding women's role? Have your views changed since then or remained the same? Why?

2. Discuss the role of tradition. How many of our attitudes/practices regarding this issue are based on tradition rather than Scripture? What makes it difficult to tell the difference between the two?

3. What do you think of the original position statement of Maury Hills? Is it too freeing or too restrictive? Why?

WOMEN IN THE CREATION STORY

Warning. You are going to be tempted to skip these next four chapters and jump straight to the controversial texts. Please do not do this. The next four chapters are critical to understanding what the Bible actually says about women's role. We cannot allow our views to be shaped by only one or two passages (which are often taken out of context). We must allow our view to be shaped by the whole of Scripture.

The creation story is foundational to how we interpret men and women's roles in the church. How we understand the first three chapters of Genesis is important to how we understand the rest of Scripture, especially since Paul references creation in both controversial texts on women's role. Of course, egalitarians see nothing in the creation story to suggest leadership is exclusive to males, while many complementarians do. Let's take a look.

> *Then God said, "Let us make mankind in our image, in our likeness, so that they may rule over the fish in the sea and the birds in the sky, over the livestock and all the wild animals, and over all the creatures that*

> *move along the ground." So God created mankind in his own image, in the image of God he created them; male and female he created them. God blessed them and God said to them, "Be fruitful and increase in number; fill the earth and subdue it. Rule over the fish in the sea and the birds in the sky and over every living thing that moves on the ground."*
> *-Genesis 1:26-28*

A couple of important points here. First, both male and female are made in the image of God (v. 27). Second, both male and female are given dominion over the earth (v. 28). Both are commanded to rule over the earth and subdue it. This is not an exclusive male right as is sometimes taught. It was given to both genders. As John Mark Hicks points out in his book *Women Serving God*, in Genesis 1 there is no distinction between the genders other than the mention there was "male and female." Otherwise, no order or differentiated roles are suggested. Both are created equally and given the same commands. Men and women have a shared identity and a shared vocation.

> *The Lord God said, 'It is not good for the man to be alone. I will make a helper suitable for him.*
> *-Genesis 2:18*

The word that catches our attention in English translations is "helper." It seems to indicate subordination. However, the Hebrew word is *ezer* and is the same word used in other places in the Old Testament to describe God. He is called a "helper" to humans and that certainly does not make him subordinate to us. This word is best understood as one who complements man or completes man. The NRSV is helpful here in its rendering of Genesis 2:18 as *"It is not good that the man should be alone, I will make him a helper as his partner."* The idea is partnership not subordination.

> *So the Lord God caused the man to fall into a deep sleep; and while he was sleeping, he took one of the man's ribs and then closed up the place with flesh. Then the Lord God made a woman from the rib he had taken out of the man, and he brought her to the man. The man said, "This is now bone of my bones, and flesh of my flesh; she shall be called woman, because she was taken out of man." That is why a man leaves his father and his mother and is united to his wife, and they become one flesh.*
>
> *-Genesis 2:21-24*

All this teaches us is that man was created first and woman was created from man. Is that of any significance? Maybe. Keep reading.

> *When the woman saw that the fruit of the tree was good for food and pleasing to the eye, and also desirable for gaining wisdom, she took some and ate it. She also gave some to her husband, who was with her, and he ate it.*
>
> *-Genesis 3:6*

Interesting side note. I was always under the impression the woman and the serpent were alone. In other words, Adam was off in another part of the garden while the serpent tempted the woman. She ate it, then went and found Adam, and tempted him to eat. This is not what the text says. Eve and Adam were together. She ate first, but Adam was right there with her the whole time. Both sinned and both suffered the consequences. There is no distinction (at least in Genesis) that one was any worse than the other.

Both are given consequences for their sin and here is the specific consequence given to the woman:

> *I will make your pains in childbearing very severe; with painful labor you will give birth to children. Your desire will be for your husband, and he will rule over you.*
>
> -Genesis 3:16

This is the first and only mention in the creation story of man ruling woman. What does it mean? Does it bear any weight on future women's roles in the church? Here's a quick summary of the way the two sides understand it:

- **Egalitarians** – Say the act of male dominion and female submission is a direct result of the Fall. It was not God's original intent. He created male and female equal and in perfect partnership, but as a result of sin, the male began to dominate and the roles become unequal. Jesus came to redeem the original intent of creation. Therefore, in God's kingdom there is no male and female, but all are one in Christ Jesus (Gal 3:28).

- **Complementarians** – Say the act of male headship and female submission is something that existed prior to the Fall. This was part of God's original plan as evidenced by the order of creation. Adam was created first and then Eve was created. So, what happened at the Fall was not the establishment of different roles, but a perversion of those roles. Before sin, the two existed in perfect partnership where male leadership was not about ruling but about serving. After the Fall, the roles of men and women became corrupted. Jesus came to redeem creation and reestablish the created order of things. Not the doing away of male/female differences but the intent that men lead in the right spirit and the women submit in the right spirit (Eph 4).

Where does that leave us? I think creation points more to equality than some of us were originally led to believe. John Mark Hicks says we read "male authority" or "male headship" into the text because we read with 1st Timothy 2 in mind. As he puts it, *"there is no hint of any rank or authority in Genesis 2 unless we read Genesis 2 through the lens of a particular interpretation of Paul's words."* It is simply not there. But what about the rest of the Old Testament? How were women viewed in ancient Israel?

DISCUSSION QUESTIONS

1. Why is it important to start with the creation story instead of skipping ahead to the controversial texts in the New Testament?

2. Did you learn anything new in his chapter about the role of men and women at creation? If so, what?

3. How do you feel about the order of creation and consequences of the Fall? Which explanation resonates more with you - Egalitarian or Complementarian?

WOMEN IN THE OLD TESTAMENT

When you read past Genesis 3 you notice a few things in the Old Testament. One, the oppressed condition of females. Within its pages are stories of physical abuse, sexual abuse, polygamy, economic exploitation, etc. These are the effects of the Fall and examples of how sin affected the treatment of women in ancient Israel. However, there are also many protections within the Hebrew Scriptures that were not commonplace for the time.

For example, nowhere in the Old Testament were women considered property as they were in other neighboring societies. Instead, the Bible teaches they were created in the image of God as a partner, not a servant or slave. In Proverbs 31, the Bible describes women as people who are to be respected, valued, and praised. In Exodus and Leviticus, children are instructed to obey and honor their Mother as well as their Father. In Deuteronomy, there are protections for women concerning divorce and Numbers says in the absence of male heirs, women were permitted to receive the family's inheritance and own property. These are all examples of how the Hebrew

Scriptures present women in a much more positive light than most other ancient documents.

There are also examples of several women who played pivotal roles in the Old Testament story and some who served in prominent leadership roles. It is just that we did not hear much about them in Vacation Bible School. In VBS, all the great heroes of the Bible were male, but there were several prominent female heroes in the Old Testament story as well. For example:

- Miriam led the people in worship after the parting of the Red Sea (Exo 15:20).

- Deborah led as a judge ("official leader") in ancient Israel (Jud 4:4, 5:7).

- Huldah prophesied concerning Scripture in the time of King Josiah (2nd Kgs 22:14).

In addition, there are women like Sarah, Rahab, Ruth, Hannah, and Esther who were considered examples of the faith or leaders of the faith. Granted, there are many more examples of male leadership in the Old Testament, but it was a patriarchal society. What is significant is even in a society like this, there is no Hebrew text that silences women in assemblies or prohibits women from serving in leadership roles.

Conservative scholar Craig Bloomberg points out that women could serve in *any of the public leadership roles* in Israel except for one. Women were not allowed to serve as priests. Only Aaron and his male descendants could serve in that office.

Is this important? Complementarians say, "Yes! It supports the principle of male headship." Egalitarians say, "No! It was merely a cultural accommodation." Who's right? Let's keep going.

DISCUSSION QUESTIONS

1. If you grew up attending VBS or going to Sunday School, how many stories did you hear about the female heroes of the Old Testament? Were they as well-known as the male heroes? If not, why not?

2. The Old Testament contains several protections for women that were not commonplace in ancient society. Yet, it also contains many stories of abuse and exploitation of women. How do we reconcile this?

3. Do you believe the restriction of not allowing women to serve as priests is more connected to created order or cultural accommodation?

WOMEN IN THE TIME OF JESUS

Jesus ministered in the life of Israel so perhaps this chapter should have been folded into the last one. However, the practice of the Jewish faith in Jesus' time looked different than the time of Moses. In the Intertestamental period, views shifted in regard to women and many of the restrictions tightened. This was largely due to the Scribes and Pharisees. They begin to teach that women could not be taught the Torah by themselves or in the company of men. Women could not communicate the teaching the Torah to others (not even their own children). Women could not be a disciple of a Rabbi and in some cases, they even forbid Rabbis from speaking with women in public. None of these were consistent with Old Testament teaching. They were simply rules taught by men and Jesus challenged every one of them.

The Gospels portray a remarkably positive and inclusive view of women (especially considering the time period). Women are listed in the genealogy of Jesus, given prominence in the birth story, appear as main characters in the parables, recognized as great examples of faith, among the first disciples of Jesus, appear as the main financial backers of Jesus' ministry, and are the first witnesses to the resurrection. Jesus set a radical new precedent in regard to women. He treated them with dignity and respect and welcomed them into his circle. He even shocked his own disciples with how inclusive he was of women (see John 4).

The Gospel of Luke gives more attention to women than any other gospel and he makes sure to point out that women were included in Jesus' ministry. Some believe it is because Luke was a Gentile and found it impressive that Jesus went out of his way to include those previously excluded by society. Perhaps this is one of the characteristics Luke admired most in Jesus—how he included everyone in his ministry even the most marginalized. There are three passages that stand out.

> *There was also a prophet, Anna, the daughter of Penuel, of the tribe of Asher. She was very old; she had lived with her husband seven years after her marriage, and then was a widow until she was eighty-four. She never left the temple but worshiped night and day, fasting and praying. Coming up to them at that very moment, she gave thanks to God and spoke about the child to all who were looking forward to the redemption of Jerusalem.*
>
> *-Luke 2:36-38*

Notice Anna was not only a prophet, but she spoke about Jesus to all who would listen. She was *a leader* and *a speaker*. In effect, the first "preacher" to share the good news about Jesus was a woman.

> *After this, Jesus traveled about from one town and village to another, proclaiming the good news of the kingdom of God. The twelve were with him, and also some women who had been cured of evil spirits and diseases: Mary (called Magdalene) from whom the seven demons had come out; Joanna the wife of Chuza, the manager of Herod's household; Susanna; and many others. These women were helping to support them out of their own means.*
>
> -Luke 8:1-3

Luke intentionally included women in the description to show that many prominent women were active in the ministry of Jesus. In fact, they funded it out of their own means. I believe Luke's intent was to affirm female dignity and show how Jesus treated women as equal persons created in the image of God, even when doing so was counter cultural. Perhaps the most powerful example of this is Luke 10:

> *As Jesus and his disciples were on their way, he came to a village where a woman named Martha opened her home to him. She had a sister called Mary, who sat at the Lord's feet listening to what he said. But Martha was distracted with all the preparations that had to be made. She came to him and asked, "Lord, don't you care that my sister has left me to do all the work by myself? Tell her to help me." "Martha, Martha," the Lord answered, "you are worried and upset about*

many things, but few things are needed—or indeed only one. Mary has chosen what is better, and it will not be taken away from her."

-Luke 10:38-42

What is going on here? I had always thought Mary was being lazy and Martha was doing all the work. This is what upset her. But there is more going on than what is immediately obvious to a modern reader. Mary was violating the cultural norms of the day. By sitting at the feet of Jesus she was assuming the posture of someone learning from a Rabbi, which was forbidden to women. Women were to be confined to the more traditional roles as exemplified by Martha, but Jesus says, *"Mary has chosen what is better, and it will not be taken away from her."* Jesus taught that women were free to come and learn from him and be disciples. This is evident from other interactions with women in the Gospels and the number of women who were present throughout his ministry.

What you see in Jesus is exactly what you would expect. He shook the cultural norms. He challenged human precepts. He affirmed women, welcomed them, respected them, and valued their contributions to the faith. However, some point out that he did not completely do away with male and female differences. Among his core leadership, the Apostles, were only males. Does that matter? Complementarians would say so. Egalitarians would say not really.

Again, who's right? Does the death, burial, and resurrection of Jesus change anything? What about the gifting of the Spirit and the start of the New Testament church? We turn our attention there next.

DISCUSSION QUESTIONS

1. "The Gospels contain a remarkably positive and inclusive view of women (especially considering the time period)." Do you agree or disagree with this statement? Have you always felt that way? Why or why not?

2. Why do you think Luke gives more attention to the role of women than any other Gospel writer? What is he trying to communicate through passages like Luke 8:1ff and Luke 10:38ff?

3. In what ways did Jesus shake the "cultural norms" regarding women's role? Can you think of other examples not mentioned in this chapter?

WOMEN IN THE NEW TESTAMENT CHURCH

The New Testament Church is critical to our understanding women's role for two reasons. One, we are still part of it. Today's church is part of the New Testament Church. Thus, their first century examples are still important to us in the twenty first century. Two, there are many positive examples of female leadership and participation in the early church.

This is surprising to a lot of people. It was to me. Like many strict complementarians, I grew up thinking the New Testament only had two things to say about women's role – "be silent" and "don't teach." I was wrong. The early church is packed with examples of women leading in ways many modern churches disallow.

Since there are many examples here, I'm going to review these passages in Q&A format. Do not rush through these verses. They are important. Spend some time here.

1. What contributions did women make in the establishment of the early church?

- **Acts 1:14** – *"They all joined together constantly in prayer, along with the women, and Mary the mother of Jesus, and with his brothers."* Both men and women were together on the day of Pentecost and women were clearly among the early disciples of Jesus.

- **Acts 2:3-4** – *"They saw what seemed to be tongues of fire that separated and came to rest of each of them. All of them were filled with the Holy Spirit and began to speak in other tongues as the Spirit enabled them."* Both men and women received the gift of the Spirit and both men and women began to speak in tongues. In other words, women were publicly proclaiming the good news of Jesus. They were gifted to speak and evangelize in the same way as men (see Acts 2:17-18 as well).

- **Acts 9:36** – *"In Joppa there was a disciple named Tabitha (in Greek her name is Dorcas); she was always doing good and helping the poor."* Tabitha is defined as a disciple in the same way as a male disciple.

- **Acts 16:14-15** – *"One of those listening was a woman from the city of Thyatira named Lydia, a dealer in purple cloth. She was a worshiper of God. The Lord opened her heart to respond to*

Paul's message. When she and her household were baptized, she invited us into her home. 'If you consider me a believer in the Lord,' she said, 'come and stay at my house.' And she persuaded us." The first convert to Christianity in this area was a woman who influenced her entire household to become Christians. Some believe this was another way of saying she hosted or lead a church in her home.

- **Acts 17:4, 12** – *"Some of the Jews were persuaded and joined Paul and Silas, as did a large number of God-fearing Greeks and quite a few prominent women... As a result, many of them believed, as did also a number of prominent Greek women and many Greek men."* Many leading women joined Paul & Silas which is consistent with much of Paul's ministry. These women joined him not just as converts, but as fellow workers in the gospel.

- **Acts 18:24-26** – *"Meanwhile a Jew named Apollos, a native of Alexandria, came to Ephesus. He was a learned man, with a thorough knowledge of the Scriptures. He had been instructed in the way of the Lord, and he spoke with great fervor and taught about Jesus accurately, though he knew only the baptism of John. He began to speak out boldly in the synagogue. When Priscilla and Aquila heard him, they invited him to their home and explained to him the way of God more accurately."* Pricilla and Aquila are mentioned six times in the New

Testament. They were fellow workers of Paul and important to his ministry. This text tells us both explained the way of God to Apollos more accurately. Thus, this is an example of a woman teaching a man.

- **Acts 21:8-9** – *"Leaving the next day, we reached Caesarea and stayed at the house of Philip the evangelist, one of the Seven. He had four unmarried daughters who prophesied."* Other translations refer to Philip's daughters as "prophetesses." We know women served this function in the Old Testament and here is the second example of women serving this function in the New Testament time period.

2. Could women serve as evangelists (i.e. ministers) or missionaries in the early church?

- **Romans 16:3-5** – *"Greet Priscilla and Aquila, my co-workers in Christ Jesus. They risked their lives for me. Not only I but all the churches of Gentiles are grateful to them. Greet also the church that meets at their house."* This is the same couple from Acts 18, and they are referred to here as "co-workers" of Paul. If you scan down the page to verse 21 you see it is the same phrase used to describe Timothy who was clearly recognized as a minister in that day and age. Thus, Paul uses the term "co-worker" to refer to both men and women. There was also a church meeting in their home.

- **Romans 16:6-7** – *"Greet Mary, who worked very hard for you. Greet Andronicus and Junia, my fellow Jews who have been in prison with me. They are outstanding among the apostles, and they were in Christ before I was."* Andronicus and Junia may be another couple similar to Priscilla and Aquila, but he refers to them as "outstanding among the apostles." Some believe Paul is referring to them as apostles. Not in the same sense as the Twelve, but in the sense of "sent by God." Others believe Paul was saying they were considered outstanding in the opinion of the apostles (referencing the Twelve). Either way, Junia seems to be recognized as a female leader in some capacity.

- **Philippians 4:2-3** – *"I plead with Euodia and I plead with Syntyche to be of the same mind in the Lord. Yes, and I ask you, my true companion, help these women since they have contended at my side in the cause of the gospel, along with Clement and the rest of my co-workers, whose names are in the book of life."* Again, Paul describes women as "co-workers" and recognizes them for sharing in his struggle in "the cause of Christ" indicating an important connection to this ministry.

- **Colossians 4:15** – *"Give my greetings to the brothers and sisters at Laodicea, and to Nympha and the church in her house."* Another woman who hosted a church in her home and several scholars believe those who hosted churches were not just hosts, but also provided some level of leadership for those churches as patrons.

3. What about the Christian assembly? Could women speak?

- **1ˢᵗ Corinthians 11:4-5, 13** – *"Every man who prays or prophesies with his head covered dishonors his head. But every woman who prays or prophesies with her head uncovered dishonors her head... Judge for yourselves: Is it proper for a woman to pray to God with her head uncovered?"* Paul is instructing the church about head coverings here but notice what is happening. Women are speaking (praying and prophesying) in the assembly. He does not address the fact that they are speaking, but only how to go about it properly.

4. Could women serve as deacons?

- **1ˢᵗ Timothy 3:11** – *"In the same way, the women are to be worthy of respect, not malicious talkers but temperate and trustworthy in everything."* There are qualities listed for both males and females here. The Greek word can be translated "women" or "wives" depending on context. I think women makes more sense here because it would not make sense to address qualifications for "deacon's wives" but not for "elder's wives." It makes more sense that he is listing qualifications for women deacons.

- **Romans 16:1** – *"I commend to you our sister Phoebe, a deacon of the church in Cenchreae."* The word for "deacon" is the Greek word *diakonos*. It can also be translated as a "minister" or "servant." It is the exact same word translated as "deacon" in 1st Timothy 3 where Paul lists the qualifications for a deacon. Pheobe was serving as a deacon in the church.

Now, a little bonus for any of you with a Church of Christ background. Have you studied your history? Early in the Restoration Movement the belief that women could serve as deacons was the predominant view. In 1827, Alexander Campbell wrote that early Christians in Jerusalem *"appointed female deacons, or deaconesses, to visit and wait upon the sisters."* And in 1835, he said, *"it appears that females were constituted deaconesses in the primitive church. Duties to females, as well as to males, demand this."*

Tolbert Fanning and W.K. Pendleton were other prominent preachers and editors who agreed with Campbell. In 1848, Pendleton said it was *"generally regarded among our brethren, as an essential element in the restoration of primitive order, to ordain, in every church, both deacons and deaconesses."*

5. What about an Elder? Can a woman serve as an Elder?

Ah-ha. That is the big question, and since it is such a big part of the discussion in 1st Timothy 2:12ff we'll save our answer for that chapter.

DISCUSSION QUESTIONS

1. Are you surprised at the long list of positive examples of women leadership in the New Testament? Why or why not?

2. Read the instructions in 1st Corinthians 11:1ff. Do you believe both men and women were praying and prophesying (i.e. speaking) in the assembly at Corinth? If so, why do some churches limit this activity today?

3. Consider the house church concept. Do you think women's role issues would be less controversial if today's church met in house churches (more akin to small groups) than our current format (pew & pulpit)? Why or why not?

SHOULD WOMEN REMAIN SILENT?
Understanding 1ˢᵗ Corinthians 14:34-35

If you skipped the other chapters and jumped straight to this one, please go back and read the others first. One of the biggest mistakes we make regarding women's role is limiting our understanding to just two seemingly restrictive passages. The full weight of Scripture must be allowed to speak to this issue.

Of course, if you did read the preceding chapters then you are probably asking a few questions. Namely, if the Bible speaks so positively and inclusively of women's participation in all these other places then how should we understand verses like 1ˢᵗ Corinthians 14:34 and 1ˢᵗ Timothy 2:12? Good question. Let's dive in.

In his first letter to the Corinthians Paul writes:

> *Women should remain silent in the churches. They are not allowed to speak, but must be in submission, as the law says. If they want to inquire about something,*

> *they should ask their own husbands at home; for it is disgraceful for a woman to speak in the church.*
> *-1ˢᵗ Corinthians 14:34-35*

Well, there you go. I'm sorry for wasting your time. I should have just quoted these two verses at the start and been done. It could have been a very short book. After all, that is what many Christians do. And yes, on the surface, these verses do seem pretty straightforward. Women are not to speak in church. If we interpret these words strictly, it means in everything. They cannot speak, sing, or even ask a question in the assembly. They should ask their husbands at home.

It also seems there are no distinctions here between the Sunday morning assembly and a Bible class, small group, or children's Sunday School class (distinctions many strict complementarians make to allow women to speak in the latter gatherings). But according to a strict reading of these two verses, women must be completely silent in all activities of the church. That is just what the Bible says. Case closed right?

Not so fast. That is what the Bible says *if* we pull those two verses out of context and read them as stand-alone instructions, but there are two major problems with this approach:

> 1. Rubel Shelly correctly asserts, *"Taken at face value, without any qualification of any sort, these two verses require more than any church is willing to demand."* I know of no congregation that strictly or consistently applies this teach-

ing. Even in strict complementarian churches there are a whole litany of exceptions to the rule and the exceptions often require dizzying logic.

2. We cannot pull these verses out of context! This violates the number one rule of Biblical interpretation—always read it in context. There was an original audience and an original intent for writing. So, we cannot possibly understand the meaning of a text for us today until we understand its original meaning. As Gordan Fee and Douglas Stuart put it in their classic book on how to interpret the Bible—*"The text can never mean to us what it never meant to them."* In other words, good hermeneutics are always rooted in good exegesis.

I know those are big fancy theological words and they sound heady. They aren't. We exegete passages all the time. For example, how many of your churches practice foot-washing? Why not? Doesn't the Bible clearly tell us to do it in John 13:14-15? It is right there in black and white. How could we ignore the clear command of this text? Because we have exegeted it.

We understand foot washing was a practice unique to that particular time and place. We still observe the principle Jesus teaches (i.e. serving others) without trying to impose the specific application to their cultural setting (i.e. washing feet). Sometimes it actually makes sense to *not* do something the Bible *clearly* commands us to do. This is not because we are ignoring the Bible. It is because we are interpreting the Bible. Now, about those two big words. A couple of definitions are in order. Exegesis is about discovering the original intended meaning of the text. What the text is saying for "then and there." Hermeneutics is about discovering the meaning for us today. What the text is saying for "here and now." Both are needed for a proper understanding of the Bible, but the order is important. We cannot correctly understand a text's meaning to us today (hermeneutics) without first understanding its original intended meaning (exegesis).

Exegesis requires that every verse of Scripture be interpreted in light of its authorship, language, literary style, cultural setting and historical situation. This is about context, and when it comes to interpretation, context is everything. This is also a great challenge of Biblical interpretation. How do we determine what is specific to them in their time and place and what is binding for all times and places? How do we determine what is cultural (i.e. temporary) and what is eternal (i.e. binding)? The only way is with good exegesis. If we try to apply these verses without exegeting them we make a huge mistake.

To begin exegeting 1st Corinthians 14:34-35, we have to ask some basic questions of the text.

1. What is the literary genre?
2. Who wrote it?
3. Who were they writing it to?
4. When was it written?

5. And, most importantly, what is going on? What prompted the author to write the things they wrote? What was the author's original intent and meaning?

If you have a good study Bible, most of this information is found in the introduction to the book. You can also find it in a Bible commentary or dictionary. Here are some quick answers on the first letter to the Corinthians:

1. It is a letter or epistle. This means the document is occasional in nature (it was written at a specific time to a specific audience for a specific purpose). Something was going on that prompted the writing and proper exegesis helps us discover what it was.
2. The apostle Paul wrote the letter.
3. He wrote it to the church (or churches) in the city of Corinth.
4. It was written somewhere near AD 55 toward the end of Paul's time in Ephesus.

All of this, with the exception of date, can actually be determined from the first two verses of the letter. 1st Corinthians 1:1-2 reveals who wrote the letter, who he wrote it to and, if we keep reading, we find out *why* he wrote it:

I appeal to you, brothers and sisters, in the name of our Lord Jesus Christ, that all of you agree with one

> *another in what you say and that there be no divisions, but that you be perfectly united in mind and thought. My brothers and sisters, some from Chole's household have informed me that there are quarrels among you. What I mean is this: One of you says, 'I follow Paul;' another, "I follow Apollos;" another, "I follow Cephas;" still another, "I follow Christ."*
>
> -1st Corinthians 1:10-12

In other words, the church was divided. There were quarrels and bickering. They were aligning behind different teachers, and different doctrines, and allowing those differences to come between their unity in Christ. Sound familiar? Sadly, yes. The church has always tended to split into warring factions over issues.

This was the reason for Paul's letter. He was trying to bring unity to a divided church. This is the larger context of the two verses in question (1st Cor 14:34-35). Something was going on, the church was divided, and Paul was trying to bring unity. Exactly what was going on? Well, starting in chapter 11, we learn that some of the disunity centers around what happens in the worship assembly.

> *Every man who prays or prophesies with his head covered dishonors his head. But every woman who prays or prophesies with her head uncovered dishonors her head – it is the same as having her head shaved. For if a woman does not cover her head, she might as well have her hair cut off; but if it is a disgrace for a*

> *woman to have her hair cut off or her head shaved, then she should cover her head... Judge for yourselves: Is it proper for a woman to pray to God with her head uncovered? Does not the very nature of things teach you that if a man has long hair, it is a disgrace to him, but that if a woman has long hair, it is her glory? For long hair is given to her as a covering. If anyone wants to be contentious about this, we have no other practice – nor do the churches of God."*
> *-1st Corinthians 11:4-6, 13-16*

Apparently, the women in Corinth were praying and prophesying in the assembly without their heads covered and Paul is correcting them here. Two things immediately jump out:

1. Women were required to wear head coverings which begs the question – why do we ignore this command today? Few modern churches require women's head coverings in the assembly, nor are women required to keep their hair long. Why not? Both commands are right here in 1st Corinthians 11. Are these churches ignoring God's Word? No, they are interpreting God's Word. Long hair and head coverings are cultural practices no longer applicable to today's church.

2. Paul is addressing an assembly and he acknowledges that women are speaking (praying and prophesying) in this assembly. Why would he do this if he believes this is forbid-

den? Wouldn't he tell them to just "be silent" instead of instructing them on how to speak properly?

Chapter 11 is the main thing that made me rethink my understanding of chapter 14. If Paul meant for women to never speak in an assembly, then why wouldn't he state it here in chapter 11? In this chapter, he is not concerned with *what* women are doing but *how* they are doing it. He is fine with women speaking in the assembly as long as it's done in the right way. This is an important distinction. The same author wrote the latter verses in chapter 14. We have to understand the meaning of 14:34 within the meaning of 11:5 and vice versa. In chapter 11, he is not concerned with women speaking in the assembly, but only that is done properly and in good order. This is because Paul's main concern here (and in the chapters that follow) is order in the assembly.

Remember the larger context. The church is divided. One of the sources of division is what happened in the worship assembly. Paul addresses this division in chapters 11-14. In chapter 11, he deals with head coverings and the abuse of the Lord's Supper. In chapter 12, he talks about the practice of spiritual gifts and diversity within the body of Christ. In chapter 13, he appeals to the higher standard (love). And finally, in chapter 14, he addresses specific instructions for speaking in tongues and prophecy concluding with a general appeal for order in the assembly. We have to understand the verses in question (14:34-35) within this larger context.

> *What then shall we say, brothers and sisters? When you come together, each of you has a hymn, or a word of instruction, a revelation, a tongue, or an interpretation. Everything must be done so that the church may be built up. If anyone speaks in a tongue, two – or at most three – should speak, one at a time, and someone must interpret. If there is no interpreter, the speaker should keep quiet in the church and speak to himself and to God.*
>
> *-1ˢᵗ Corinthians 14:26-28*

Notice he tells a specific group in the church to "be quiet." Those who speak in tongues without an interpreter should be quiet. But in this case, as with later cases, the silence is conditional. If there is no interpreter, they should be silent.

If there is, they are free to speak.

> *Two or three prophets should speak, and the others should weigh carefully what is said. And if a revelation comes to someone who is sitting down, the first speaker should stop. For you can all prophesy in turn so that everyone may be instructed and encouraged.*
>
> *-1ˢᵗ Corinthians 14:29-31*

Again, he told another specific group in the church to stop talking and be silent. Again, it is conditional. If a revelation comes to someone who is sitting down, the speaker should stop and allow them to share. If not, the speaker may continue.

> *The spirits of prophets are subject to the control of prophets. For God is not a God of disorder but of peace – as in all congregations of the Lord's people.*
> *-1ˢᵗ Corinthians 14:32-33*

These two verses represent the main thesis of Paul in chapters 11-14. He appeals to unity by appealing to order. He does this in the context of those speaking in tongues, those prophesying, and women. In each case, he is appealing to order in the assembly and asking for a conditional silence. Now, before we hit the next two verses let's talk about the punctuation here. Some translations attach the phrase "as in all churches of the saints" to v. 34 and some attach it to v. 33. That little punctuation mark makes a big difference. Is he saying all churches of the saints should be orderly or all churches of the saints should not allow women to talk? Since the Greek did not include punctuation translators have to interpret. I think it makes more sense to attach the phrase "as in all congregations of the Lord's people" with v. 33 because it better fits his overall thesis. Things are out of order in the church in Corinth and he is appealing for order and peace.

> *Women should remain silent in the churches. They are not allowed to speak, but must be in submission, as the law says. If they want to inquire about something, they should ask their own husbands at home; for it is disgraceful for a woman to speak in church. Or did the word of God originate with you? Or are you the only people it has reached? If anyone thinks they are a prophet or otherwise gifted by the Spirit, let*

> *them acknowledge that what I am writing to you is the Lord's command. But if anyone ignores this, they will themselves be ignored. Therefore, my brothers and sisters, be eager to prophesy, and do not forbid speaking in tongues. But everything should be done in a fitting and orderly way.*
>
> -1st Corinthians 14:34-40

Two points of interest. One, it is still a conditional silence (if... then). Two, it is interesting that many Church of Christ and Baptist Churches strictly apply v. 34 ("women should remain silent") but have no problem skipping over v. 39 ("do not forbid speaking in tongues"). It is because they interpret v. 39 as specific to that time and place, but v. 34 as not. Why not?

Here is what I think is going on based on the available clues. Paul's primary concern is order in the assembly. He starts and ends the entire section by appealing to order in the assembly because the assemblies are in chaos. It is within that context he instructs women to be silent suggesting that perhaps the Corinthian women, or the Corinthian wives, (the Greek word can mean either "women" or "wives") should be silent.

It is possible the Corinthian wives were being disruptive in some way. Maybe they were asking unlearned questions (which explains v. 35), or maybe they were speaking out of turn, or practicing tongues improperly, or gossiping. We do not know exactly what was going on, but in some way the Corinthian wives were contributing to the chaos, so he instructs them to be quiet and ask questions of their husbands at home.

I believe Carroll Osborn gets it right when he says:

> *The real issue is not the extent to which a woman may participate in the work and worship of the church, but the manner. Paul's corrective does not ban women from speaking in worship, but stops the disruptive verbal misconduct of certain wives who are giving free reign to 'irresistible impulses' to 'pipe up' at will with questions in the assembly by redirecting these questions to another setting where they can gain access to information without causing chaos…1st Corinthians 14:34-35 teaches that these particular wives, like the uncontrolled tongue-speakers and prophets at Corinth, must defer to the assembly by voluntarily yielding to orderliness. The general principle that is to be applied to contemporary church life is that decorum is mandatory for all in the public assembly without regard for gender.*

I do not see anything in 14:34-35 that prohibits a woman from speaking in an assembly. The instruction seems specific to that particular time and place. Something was going on that prompted him to tell the Corinthian wives to be quiet, but there is no reason to think he meant it as an eternally binding command for all churches in all times.

DISCUSSION QUESTIONS

1. "Taken at face value, without any qualifications of any sort, this passage requires more than anyone is willing to demand." Do you agree or disagree with this statement? Why? Can you think of other passages in the Bible where the same thing is true?

2. How do you determine if a passage is cultural (i.e. only binding to that day and time) or eternal (i.e. binding to all days and times)?

3. When it comes to understanding context and the author's original intent is it possible to have 100% certainty? If not, does that bother you? If God knew we would debate the meaning of these passages why didn't he spell it out more clearly?

ARE WOMEN PERMITTED TO TEACH?
Understanding 1st Timothy 2:12-13

Let's take a little quiz. Find a piece of paper and number it one through seven. Scot McKnight developed this quiz, and he gave it to his college-level Bible classes every year. He isolated the seven basic commands in 1st Timothy 2:8-15 and asked his students to determine whether or not the command should still be practiced by Christians today. Just answer each question with a simple "yes" or "no." Should this command still be practiced by Christians today?

1. Males must pray with their hands lifted up (2:8).
2. Males must pray without anger or disputing (2:8).
3. Women must dress modestly (2:9).
4. Women must not have elaborate hairstyles, wear gold, pearls, or expensive clothing (2:9).
5. Women must have good deeds (2:10).

6. Women must be silent and quiet (2:11, 12).

7. Women must not teach or have authority (2:12).

I have given this quiz to several groups over the years and after everyone finished writing down their answers, I asked them two questions: One, how many of you answered "yes" to every single question (100% of the commands are binding)? Two, how many of you answered "no" to every single question (none of the commands are binding)? No one raises a hand to either question.

This is exactly what you would expect because the answer lies somewhere in between. As much as we respect Scripture, we do not think all of it applies to today. Obviously, some of it speaks just to their day and time and some of it speaks to all days and times. There are certainly some theological principles and commands that remain binding on Christians today. Thus, we have the supreme challenge of interpreting New Testament letters. What is cultural and what is binding? What still applies to Christians today and what does not?

How can we possibly answer those questions? Only with good exegesis. We have to exegete these passages and understand their historical context before we try to apply them to a modern context. And, like the letter to the Corinthians, many of the answers are right here in the beginning of the letter:

Paul, an apostle of Christ Jesus by the command of God our Savior and of Christ Jesus our hope, To

> *Timothy my true son in the faith: Grace, mercy and peace from God the Father and Christ Jesus our Lord.*
> *-1st Timothy 2:1-2*

Paul is the author of this letter, and he wrote it to Timothy. We know Paul was a mentor to Timothy. In Acts 16, we read about their relationship and learn Timothy was a traveling companion and co-worker of Paul. In Acts 20, we learn that Paul left Timothy in Ephesus to build up the church there. He left him there for a reason.

> *As I urged you when I went into Macedonia, stay there in Ephesus so that you may command certain people not to teach false doctrines any longer or to devote themselves to myths and endless genealogies. Such things promote controversial speculations rather than advancing God's work—which is by faith. The goal of this command is love, which comes from a pure heart and a good conscience and a sincere faith. Some have departed from these and have turned to meaningless talk. They want to be teachers of the law, but they do not know what they are talking about or what they so confidently affirm.*
> *-1st Timothy 2:3-7*

There was something going on in Ephesus. False teachers were distorting the faith and stirring up controversy. So, everything Paul says after this must be heard through this lens. The above verses are *why* he is writing the letter. They are *why* he gives instructions on worship in the next chapter (to both men and women). They are *why* he gives instructions on choosing leaders in the chapter after that. It is all motivated by Paul's desire to combat these false teachers. We must hear his instructions throughout the entire letter within this specific context.

> *"I urge, then, first of all, that petitions, prayers, intercession and thanksgiving be made for all people—for kings and all those in authority, that we may live peaceful and quiet lives in all godliness and holiness. This is good, and pleases God our Savior, who wants all people to be saved and to come to a knowledge of the truth.*
> *-1st Timothy 2:1-4*

This is Paul's thesis here—pray for all people, live good and holy lives in quietness and peace so that people would come to a saving knowledge of God. He then gives more specific instructions to men and women:

> *Therefore, I want men everywhere to pray, lifting up holy hands without anger or disputing. I also want the women to dress modestly, with decency and propriety, adorning themselves, not with elaborate hairstyles or gold or pearls or expensive clothes, but with good deeds, appropriate for women who profess to worship God. A woman should learn in quietness and full submission. I do not permit a woman to teach or to assume authority over a man; she must be quiet.*
> *-1st Timothy 2:8-12*

The last two verses garner the most attention (vs. 11-12). Is he giving a universal, timeless command to the church concerning woman teaching or is he giving a specific, temporal command to address the situation in Ephesus? This is the question up for debate. However, little of it centers around verse 11. The word for "quietness" used here is the same as the one used in verse 2. It does not refer to "silence" or "not speaking." It refers to attitude and humility. Some feel there is a direct connection to context here. Perhaps the false teachers in Ephesus were women? Or perhaps the women who had not yet been properly taught were more susceptible to the deception of the false teachers? Either way, in verse 11, he is simply addressing *how* women should learn.

Verse 12 is more troublesome. This is the "clobber verse" historically used by strict complementarians to silence women's voices in the church. However, just like 1st Corinthians 14:34, it is not as simple as it seems. The Greek word for "authority" can mean one of two things. In a negative sense, it means "to domineer over." Some feel there may have been women exercising their freedom to speak in the assembly but doing it in a domineering way and that is specifically what Paul is prohibiting here. It is not a universal command against teaching but addresses the improper way teaching was being done in Ephesus. In a positive sense, the word means "to govern." So, others feel Paul is prohibiting women from governing and thus, by extension, teaching.

It is not entirely clear from this passage alone. Some see this text as a general prohibition against women teaching while others suggest Paul more concerned with how they teach. The question again comes down to cultural or binding. Is Paul providing these instructions on women's teaching for that specific time and place because of what was happening in the church of Ephesus or is he providing instructions for the church in all times and places? This is where the interpretation of verses 13-15 comes in.

> *For Adam was formed first, then Eve. And Adam was not the one deceived; it was the woman who was deceived and became a sinner. But women will be saved through childbearing—if they continue in faith, love and holiness with propriety.*
> *-1ˢᵗ Timothy 2:13-15*

A good complementarian would say, "Ah-ha, see it is binding for all time because Paul connects it to the created order of things." A good egalitarian would say, "No, this is more of an analogy of the present situation. He is explaining not prescribing." In other words, there are women being deceived by false teachers. Paul compares them to Eve and cautions them not to teach or exercise authority until they have been properly taught themselves.

Complementarians would say, "No. The created order is important because man is supposed to be head of woman." There are certainly other places in the Bible they can go to support this line of reasoning, but the argument does not always hold up. For example:

1. There is nothing in the original account of creation that suggests order equals authority. Both male and female are considered equal partners in Genesis 2. Man is "head" of woman but perhaps this is better understood "source." Thus, man is the "source" of woman (she was created from his rib) yet woman is the "source" of man (he was born from her womb). This helps make sense of verse 15 which is an admittedly confusing verse.

2. Paul used the same created order argument in 1st Corinthians 11 regarding head coverings, yet we have determined this is cultural. Few women in the church today are forced to wear head coverings or keep their hair long because of "the created order of things."

3. The idea of order equaling authority has problems elsewhere because in other places in the New Testament Paul used this same line of reasoning for why slaves should submit to their masters. In that case we rightly determined there is a higher theological principle which trumps the cultural concession. I believe the same is true with women's role.

I must confess. I have changed my mind on 1st Timothy 2:12. When I originally taught this series in 2010, I leaned towards the understanding that Paul was prohibiting "authoritative teaching" by women. He was not prohibiting all forms of teaching by a woman, but a specific kind of teaching limited to the elders of a church. Thus, Paul was prohibiting women from serving as elders which makes 1st Timothy 2:12 fit with the following verses in 1st Timothy 3:1-7.

However, this argument has not held up to scrutiny and I now see the verses much more through the lens of the false teachers in 1st Timothy 1:3-4. There was something going on with false teachers in Ephesus and it seems the women were involved somehow. It is not exactly clear how, but because of their involvement Paul is instructing them not to teach or exercise authority. Not as an eternally binding command on the church, but as a specific temporal command to address the situation in Ephesus. This makes more sense to me in light of the context of the letter.

That said, I recognize this passage is not easily interpreted and there are two acceptable choices for understanding it. One, Paul's teaching is historically conditioned and not universal or timeless (the position I just outlined above). Two, Paul's teaching is unaffected by the historical context and therefore applicable to every age of the church.

The big question here is why? Why would we bind this command in verse 12 when the other commands immediately preceding it are considered cultural? And I understand Paul connects it to creation in verses 14-15 but I also understand that the meaning of these verses is not entirely clear. At the end of the day, you will have to reach your own conclusions.

One more confession. While my individual position has changed since the original study in 2010 our church's official position has not. We still do not have women serving as elders at Maury Hills Church. But why not?! Why the disconnect? Well, it's really not. I readily admit this passage should give us pause and there is at least enough uncertainty here to remind us to hold our views loosely and not too dogmatically. I also recognize I am one individual in a body of believers who may well have different views on this issue. This explains why our church has not yet changed our position on women elders.

1st Timothy 2:12 gives us pause and we do not have complete unity in our understanding. Some of our current elders are egalitarian and others are complementarian (same for our members). So, we continue to study and pray together over this issue. While doing so, women continue to participate in every activity of the assembly (including preaching) and serve in any capacity in the church with the exception of elder. We fully admit this is not a perfect solution and it frustrates people on both sides of the issue. It is simply an example of a church trying to work through differing interpretations on a controversial issue while maintaining unity. Those of us who are egalitarian can at least acknowledge we are not 100% sure what Paul means here and it is possible he intends some limitations. While those who are complementarian can acknowledge he cannot mean as much limitations as we have historically understood, and it is possible that his limitations here were specific to the situation in Ephesus. In short, we both acknowledge that "we might be wrong."

Thankfully, the basis of our salvation or fellowship is not based on being right. It is based on Jesus. Period. Whenever a new member asks our position on women's role at Maury Hills Church, I give it with this caveat: If you struggle with the fact that only men serve as elders here, please be patient and give us the benefit of the doubt. If you struggle with the fact that both men and women preach here, please be patient and give us the benefit of the doubt. We will not (and do not) all agree here, but if we agree on Jesus that is enough.

DISCUSSION QUESTIONS

1. The most difficult part of taking a position on women's role is applying it consistently. Can you think of some examples where the church has been inconsistent in our application of this issue? What were some of the "unwritten rules" concerning women's role in the church you grew up in?

2. Do you believe Paul's main concern in 1st Timothy 2:11ff is whether or not women teach or how they teach? Why?

3. What do you think of Russ' confession that he has changed his mind on the meaning of 1st Timothy 2:11ff but the church has not changed its position? How is possible for churches to navigate issues like this when everyone is not in "complete unity?"

CONCLUDING REMINDERS

I know this book has not answered every question. It has not even *asked* every question! I appreciate you studying with me and want to close with three things for us to keep in mind as we try to navigate difficult passages together:

1. We seek to interpret in humility. We realize we are not the only ones trying to understand and apply the Bible and we recognize the difficulty involved.

2. We seek to interpret in community. We realize the Bible is meant to be read and understood together. Disagreements are not a source of concern. They are how we learn from each other. Reading the Bible in community helps us hear what others are saying and keep our biases in check.

3. We seek to interpret in unity. I know many may think this is impossible, but I believe it is. We should never allow what we disagree on to come between what we agree on. Unity

matters to the church because it matters to Christ. May we all, regardless of our position on this subject, seek the way of unity.

Perhaps there is no better way to end this book than by reading the prayer Jesus prayed for us. In the Garden of Gethsemane, right before Jesus went to the cross, he prayed these words:

> *My prayer is not for them alone [the disciples]. I pray also for those who will believe in me through their message, that all of them may be one, Father, just as you are in me and I am in you. May they also be in us so that the world may believe that you have sent me. I have given them the glory that you gave me, that they may be one as we are one – I in them and you in me – so that they may be brought to complete unity. Then the world will know that you sent me and have loved them even as you have loved me.*
> *-John 17:20-23*

May we answer that prayer.

DISCUSSION QUESTIONS

1. Of the "three things to keep in mind as we navigate difficult passages" which is most important to you?

2. Discuss your feelings/thoughts throughout this study. Have you changed your mind on anything? Where did this book challenge your thinking and where did it affirm it?

3. Throughout the book Russ emphasized "there are many different opinions on this issue" and "we shouldn't allow our disagreements on this issue to come between our agreement on Christ." Why is that so an important?

WORKS REFERENCED AND RESOURCES FOR FURTHER STUDY

BOOKS:
Allen, Leonard. *Distant Voices: Uncovering a Forgotten Past for a Changing Church.* 1999.

Belleville, Linda L., Craig L. Bloomberg, Craig S. Keener, Thomas R. Schreiner. *Two Views on Women in Ministry.* Zondervan. 2005. James R. Beck (editor)

Fee, Gordan, Douglas Stuart. *How to Read the Bible for All Its Worth.* Fourth Edition. 2014.

Hicks, John Mark. *Searching for the Pattern: My Journey in Interpreting Scripture.* John Mark Hicks. 2019.

Hicks, John Mark. *Women Serving God: My Journey in Understanding Their Story in the Bible.* John Mark Hicks. 2020.

McKnight, Scot. *The Blue Parakeet: Rethinking How You Read the Bible.* Zondervan. 2008.

Osborne, Carroll. *Women in the Church: Reclaiming the Ideal.* ACU Press. 2001.

ARTICLES/STUDIES:
Blazer, Dan. "The Role of Women in the Church." 13-week study taught at Brooks Ave Church of Christ (2000).

Hicks, John Mark. "Women in the Assembly: 1 Corinthians 14:34-35" https://johnmarkhicks.com/2009/02/20/women-in-the-assembly-1-corinthians-1434-35/

Hicks, John Mark. "Women Serving God: Four Bible Classes" presented at Woodmont Hills Church of Christ (2004). https://johnmarkhicks.com/2009/02/20/women-in-the-assembly-1-corinthians-1434-35/

Shelly, Rubel. "A Woman's Place Is…" *Wineskins* (Vol 2, No.1), May 1993. https://archives.wineskins.org/article/a-womans-place-is-may-1993/

SERMONS:
Cope, Mike. "Women in the Church." Message taught at the Highland Church of Christ (2005).

Robinson, Thomas. "A Community Without Barriers." A series of messages taught at the Manhattan Church of Christ (1999). http://www.communitywithoutbarriers.com/

Shelly, Rubel, John York, and Wes Crawford. "Women in God's Service." A series of messages taught at Woodmont Hills Church of Christ (2004)